Building Your Vision

Ten Steps to Starting a Business

Carlton Reed

Building Your Vision

Introduction

Dear Reader,

By picking up this book you have made the first step into becoming an entrepreneur. If you are interested in starting your own business, but clueless on the steps to begin, this is the book for you. I believe in your vision and that you are capable of reaching your dreams.

William Arthur Ward said it best "If you can imagine it, you can achieve it; if you can dream it, you can become it." This book will guide you step by step on how to start your first business and transform your vision into life. I am excited to be your guide throughout this journey. Sit back, relax, and take notes. It is time to build your vision!

I dedicate this book to you.

Carlton Reed

Building Your Vision

The Beginning

At a very young age I became fascinated about the idea of starting a business. I spent countless hours researching and studying this subject. Once I felt confident that I was ready to embark upon this journey, I got together with an investor and one of my best friends to create TeenZBuy.com a virtual retailer for teenagers.

It was one of the most challenging experiences of my life. Supported by my experiences operating a nonprofit organization I was able to navigate my way. Since TeenZBuy.com many people have reached out to me seeking insight on how to start a business. It has been my experience that the first steps in realizing your vision of a company is simply to get started.

This book has organized many of the tools and resources I have used to start my business into ten impactful steps.

"There are times when a leader must move out ahead of the flock, go off in a new direction, confident that he is leading his people the right way."

Nelson Mandela

Building Your Vision

Building Your Vision

Table of Contents

Introduction 2

The Beginning 3

Table of Contents 5

Step 1 Brainstorm 6

Step 2 Business Model Canvass 19

Step 3 Market Research 38

Step 4 Creating an One Page Business Plan 45

Step 5 Selecting a Business Structure 50

Step 6 Key Business Assets 58

Step 7 Finance Your Business 69

Step 8 Establish an Organizational Structure 91

Step 9 Market and Sell 97

Step 10 Run and Grow 115

Meet the Author 122

Bibliography 124

Building Your Vision

Step 1 Brainstorm

Building Your Vision

When you begin the process of strategic planning, visioning comes first. When visioning the business, you must think like a visionary and ask yourself, "What is my preferred future?". Draw on the beliefs, mission, and environment of the organization you envision creating. Most of the work starting a business is creative. So it's very important that you begin to exercise your creative mussels.

You can begin this by simply taking ten minutes a day sitting alone and imagining the product or service you aspire to build or manifest if you will. During this process you should ask yourself this question:

❖ What do I want to see in the future and why?
- ✓ Be specific to each area of your business; customer bassist, finances, personal prosperity, and anything else you can dream of. Remember the sky is the limit.
- ✓ Be positive and inspiring. This is just the brainstorm there is no need in stressing over the details.
- ✓ Do not assume that the business system will have the same framework as it does today in your vision. Many entrepreneurs fail because they refuse to respond to the realities of their position.

Building Your Vision

- ✓ Be open to dramatic modifications to current organization, methodology, teaching techniques, facilities, etc. However never operate without integrity to your vision. Being disingenuous to your muse will block any authentic feelings of fulfillment.

"Logic will get you from "A" to "B" imagination will get you everywhere"
~Albert Einstein~

Building Your Vision

Exercise in Creating a Vision

Take the time to assimilate this information, use the following example to exercise your planning techniques:

> It is five years from today's date and you have, marvelously enough, created your most desirable district. Now it is your job, as a team, to describe it - as if you were able to see it, realistically around you.

Respond to the following questions:

- How has the job market changed?

- What have we done to prepare our business for success in this world?

- What do we as board members spend most of our time doing?

- How are our meetings structured?

Building Your Vision

Key Components for Your Vision

Incorporate Your Beliefs

Your vision must be encompassed by your beliefs. Before you become a business owner you must understand you personal brand is your primary asset. A personal brand is the process whereby people and their careers are marked as brands. Meaning any personal action that may influence the way you are received in the business world. This includes both business and personal relationships. It will determine future business relationships. Relationships are as valuable as money because money is the energy individuals' leverage to manifest the outcomes.

Your beliefs must meet your organizational goals as well as community goals. Your business is responsible to a community of customers and employees. Aligning core beliefs with theirs is the key to running and growing a successful organization.

- ✓ Your beliefs are a statement of your values.
- ✓ Your beliefs are a public/visible declaration of your expected outcomes.
- ✓ Your beliefs must be precise and practical.

Building Your Vision

- ✓ Your beliefs will guide the actions of all involved.

- ✓ Your beliefs reflect the knowledge, philosophy, and actions of all.

- ✓ Your beliefs are a key component of strategic planning.

Create a Mission Statement

Once you have clarified your beliefs, build on them to define your mission statement which is a statement of purpose and function for your business.

- Your mission statement draws on your belief statements.

- Your mission statement must be future oriented and portray your organization as it will be, as if it already exists.

- Your mission statement must focus on one common purpose.

- Your mission statement must be specific to the organization, not generic.

- Your mission statement must be a short statement, not more than one or two sentences.

Building Your Vision

Here is an example mission statement: "By providing quality education, we empower individuals to become caring, competent, responsible citizens who value education as a lifelong process."

To come up with a statement that encompasses the major elements of your business, start with the right questions. Since you have already gone through the steps of creating your vision, answering this question should be easy for you.

Answering the following questions will help you to create a written picture of your business's mission:

1. Why are you in business?
2. What image of your business do you want to convey? Customers, suppliers, employees and the public will all have perceptions of your company. How will you create the desired picture?
3. What is (are) the products and services?
4. What level of service do you provide? Don't be vague; define what makes your service so extraordinary.
5. What roles do you and your employees play?
6. How do you differ from your competitors? Many entrepreneurs forget they are pursuing the same dollars as their competitors. What do you do better?

Building Your Vision

7. What underlying philosophies or values guided your company? This should be aligned with you personal beliefs and brand.

Putting It All Together
Like anything with lasting value, crafting a mission statement requires time, thought and planning. In fact, crafting the mission statement is as beneficial as the final statement itself because it expands the creative mind. Going through the process will help you solidify the reason for what you are doing and clarify the motivations behind your business.

Here are some tips to make your mission statement the best it can be:

- *Involve those connected to your business.* Even if you are a sole proprietor, it helps to get at least one other person's ideas for your mission statement. Other people can help you see strengths, weaknesses and voids you might miss. if you have no partners or investors to include, consider knowledgeable family members and close friends, employees or accountants. Be sure, however, to pick only positive, supportive people who truly want to see you succeed.

Building Your Vision

- *Set aside several hours--a full day, if possible--to work on your statement.* Mission statements are short--typically more than one sentence but rarely exceeding a page. Still, writing one is not a short process. It takes time to come up with language that simultaneously describes an organization's heart and soul and serves as an inspirational beacon to everyone involved in the business.
- *Plan a date.* Set aside time to meet with the people who'll be helping you. Write a list of topics to discuss or think about. Find a quiet, comfortable place away from phones and interruptions.
- *Be prepared.* If you have several people involved, be equipped with refreshments, extra lists of topics, paper and pencils. Because not everyone understand what a mission statement is about, explain its meaning and purpose before you begin.
- *Brainstorm.* Consider every idea, no matter how silly it sounds. Stimulate ideas by looking at sample mission statements and thinking about or discussing the questions in the previous section. If you're working with a group, use a flip chart to record responses so everyone can see them. Once you've finished brainstorming, ask everyone to write individual mission statements for your

Building Your Vision

business. Read the statement, select the best bits and pieces, and fit them together.

- *Use "radiant words."* Once you have the basic idea in writing, polish the language of your mission statement. "Every word counts". The statement should create dynamic, visual images and inspire action. Use offbeat, colorful verbs and adjectives to spice up your statements. Don't hesitate to drop in words like "kaleidoscope," "sizzle," "cheer," "outrageous" and "marvel" to add zest. If you want customers to boast about your goods and services, say so--along with the reasons why. Some businesses include a glossary that defines the terms used in the statement.

Once your mission statement is complete, start spreading the word! You need to convey your mission statement to others inside and outside the business to tell everyone you know where you are going and why. In due time you will be posting it in your office, where you, employees and visitors can see it every day. Print it on company materials, such as brochures and your business plan or even on the back of your business cards.

Building Your Vision

Benefits of Visioning

The process and outcomes of visioning may seem vague and superfluous. The long-term benefits are substantial, however. Visioning:

- ✓ Breaks you out of boundary thinking and opens you to a world of limitless possibilities. The infamous Steve Jobs, Founder and late Chief Executive Officer (C.E.O) of Apple Inc. built a computer technology company from a garage. Having limited resources Jobs relied on hard work and allowed his vision to pull him forward. Today Apple Inc. is one of the world's largest computer technology companies.

- ✓ Identifies direction and purpose. It is difficult to reach a destination without a location in mind. Rather than spending countless hours trying anything; having a vision focuses your attention. What you focus your attention on you will achieve.

- ✓ Results in efficiency and productivity. In business it is important to centralize all your milestones around a common goal. This will unite your team and create a sustainable work environment.

Building Your Vision

Disempowering Beliefs

As you engage in the visioning process, be alert to the following disempowering beliefs. A disempowering belief is any thought that make a person feel less than or unequal to another. Each has the capacity to destroy your progress if you are not mindful of your experiences as a leader. Here are some of the most common disempowering beliefs that hinders an entrepreneurs progress:

- Unworthiness, at time things will not work out as planned; however this is not the time to belittle yourself. We are all powerful individuals. As long as you continue to believe that you can do any good thing. It is extremely important to live with a healthy mental and spiritual body as a leader because as a leader you are responsible for the health of the company.

- Fear of failure, we all posses talents that set us apart from others. Counteractively we also have weaknesses. There is no reason to be ashamed of the progress or lack thereof within your business. You have already achieved more than most by jumping into unfamiliar territory. Now is time to leap- the net will appear!

Building Your Vision

Stay positive and trust that your hard work will pay off. Every new business owner has fears. The difference between those who make it and those who do not is there ability to persevere.

Carlton's Suggestions:

- ✓ Remember to take at least ten minutes each day creating in your mind what you wish to achieve.
- ✓ Write a clear vision and mission statement on what you intent to build moving forward.
- ✓ Keep your vision safe from negative energy.
- ✓ Starting a business is more about the long run than it is the short run. Think like a visionary plan for the future.

Building Your Vision

Step 2 Business Model Canvass

Building Your Vision

Now, that you have a clear vision of the business written down its time to generate a solid plan that the market will respond to. This is done using a Business Model Canvass. The Business Model Canvas, is a strategic management and entrepreneurial tool. It allows you to describe, design, challenge, invent, and pivot your business model. Your business model answers key question on how you will operate your business.

Step one in building a successful business is to learn what products or technologies your customers really need and are willing to buy. The vast majority of technology startups fail because too few customers buy or use their products. So don't underestimate the importance of validating and testing your ideas.

Developing the right product is hard. But what is harder is building a good business model. Fortunately, there's nothing magical about a business model. It's simply the nuts and bolts of how a business plans to generate revenue and profits. It details your long-term strategy and day-to-day operations.

Entrepreneurs put together elaborate business plans showing optimistic market-share projections. Even 1% of a billion-dollar market seems lucrative, right? Wishful thinking is great, but when it comes time to create your business model, you need to be realistic. The challenges

Building Your Vision

differ from industry to industry, but here is **Seven Basic Components of a Business Model**:

1. Reaching customers. Ralph Waldo Emerson famously said, "Build a better mousetrap, and the world will beat a path to your door." The reality is that even if you did, no one would find you. Even when you know who your prospects are, it's usually difficult and costly to reach them. You have to find them via the Internet and e-mail, or the old-fashioned way—through broadcast media, print ads, direct mail, telemarketing, or references or by cold-calling. And these potential customers are not likely to be waiting to hear from you and may not respond to you. So be sure you know how you are going to find and reach them.

2. Differentiating your product. You think you've got the very best solution, but so does the other gal (or guy). There's always competition, whether you realize it or not. Smart marketing executives know how to develop unique product-positioning strategies that highlight a product's true value. You need to thoroughly understand the competition and effectively communicate the unique advantages of your product.

3. Pricing. One of the most basic decisions you have to make is how much you're going to charge for your product or service. Giving your stuff away is the way to

Building Your Vision

go on the web, but remember that you still need to figure out how you are eventually going to make money—you can't make it up on volume. Start by understanding how much customers value what they're gaining from you. Then you need to estimate your total costs, analyze the competitive landscape, and map out your long-term strategy. For your company to survive, your product's price must be greater than its overall cost.

4. Selling. Persuading customers to buy a product that they need is one of the most important skills an entrepreneur must learn. You're going to be selling at every juncture. So you have to understand what it takes to close a deal and put together the necessary sales process. And this process has to be perfectly conceived. Be sure you test your selling strategy as you would your product.

5. Delivery/distribution. This is easy on the Internet. But for big-ticket items, you usually require a direct sales force; for mid-range products, distributors or value-added resellers; and, for low-priced items, retail outlets or the Internet. It's different in every industry and for every type of product, but you have to get this right. Your products need to be designed and packaged for the channel through which they will be distributed to customers.

Building Your Vision

6. Supporting Customers. In addition to teaching customers how to use your product, you need to ensure that you can deal with defects and returns, answer product questions, and listen to and incorporate valuable suggestions for improvement. You may need to provide consulting services to help customers integrate and implement your products. If your product is a critical component of a business, you may also need to provide 24/7 onsite or web support.

7. Achieving customer satisfaction. The ultimate success or failure of a business depends on how much it helps customers achieve their objectives. Happy customers will become your best sales people and buy more from you. Unhappy customers will become your biggest liability.

All the pieces have to come together like a jigsaw puzzle in your business model. The good news is that you don't have to start from scratch when formulating it. You can give yourself a head start by learning from competitors and other markets. It is not only the successes that provide valuable lessons; it is also the failures.

You can innovate as much in your business model as you do in your products. Be prepared to evolve your innovation strategy as you gain experience and as your market changes. Like your products, it will probably take

Building Your Vision

several versions to get your business model right; you get better with practice.

There is a large host of **Business Model Options**

Home-based

Home-based Business Drawing upon technology, you can create a legitimate and competitive business from home. It's part of our culture now, accounting for more than half of all businesses. Home-based businesses can be run full-time or part-time, and may or may not be web-based.

Upside

- ❖ **Less risk and lower startup costs** allows you to test the entrepreneurial waters without having to spend money on real estate and staff.
- ❖ **Easily scalable** you can make your home-based business as big or small as you'd like to suit existing commitments, such as parenthood and a day job.
- ❖ **Outsourcing** a great strategy to keep things simple at home. You can contract with other companies to do your public relations,

Building Your Vision

warehousing, shipping, website management, even manufacturing.

Downside

- ❖ Shipping activities and customer traffic at residential properties are restricted by local zoning ordinances (check with your local government for details).
- ❖ Working at home can come with lots of distractions and can infringe on your other domestic commitments.
- ❖ If foot traffic is necessary in your business, your home may not make the desired impression on customers.

Building Your Vision

Brick-and-Mortar

This is a business with a classic physical location outside of the home. It involves a dedicated facility whether retail, wholesale, service or manufacturing.

Upside

- Gives you an **opportunity to work face-to-face** with people and become more involved in your community.
- A **physical location** may attract walk-in traffic to supplement traffic you gain through marketing efforts, depending on your type of business.
- Gives you a **dedicated space** to go to work each day and become mentally and physically immersed in running your business.

Downside

- Higher risk and startup costs (build-out costs to set up your location, lease/purchase costs)
- Requires a full-time commitment upfront to get the facility ready for business, as well as to hire personnel to staff it.
- If your concept is retail-oriented, you must acquire inventory to merchandize your store.

Building Your Vision

E-Commerce

In this model, you don't have foot traffic in your business, only traffic to your website. You sell your product through your website to consumers or to other businesses.

Upside

- As with a home-based business, this is a lower risk, lower cost business to start. You don't necessarily need lots of personnel, inventory and facilities.
- You can choose to do it full-time or part-time.
- Easily scaleable – you can make your e-commerce business as big or small as you'd like to suit existing commitments, such as parenthood and a day job.
- You can tap into a national, or even global, customer base through the internet.

Downside

- As with a brick-and-mortar store, shipping, inventory management, and credit card processing can all become headaches if you don't

Building Your Vision

do them right, particularly if you are a one-person show.
- ❖ Over 800 million people access the internet globally, but it's a challenge to a) get that traffic to come to your site and b) convert them into a customer confident enough to make a purchase.

Franchising

When you choose a franchise business model, you use someone else's proven business concept as your entrepreneurial roadmap. Typically you pay an upfront fee, as well as a portion of revenues over time, to the franchisor.

Upside

- ❖ Lower risk than opening an independent brick-and-mortar business, because franchising provides you with a streamlined process to start your business, as well as support for marketing, business plan samples and estimates, assistance with real estate issues, and staff training.
- ❖ Provides you with a recognized, established brand to attract customers more quickly.

Building Your Vision

- To illustrate the lower risk inherent in a franchise, success rates for franchises are higher than non-franchise businesses.

Downside

- You've got to be able to pay the upfront franchise fees.
- Franchise guidelines can be strict and limit your ability to get creative with your business.
- Your financial upside is somewhat limited because you must pay your franchisor a cut of your profits.

Licensing your product

If you're working a day job and don't want to start a business, you can still take advantage of your great product idea by licensing the product to another company that has the entire infrastructure in place to properly manufacture, market and sell the product .

Upside

- Lower risk because you can work on your product part-time.

Building Your Vision

- ❖ Lower cost because your main expense is production of a prototype and testing the product to make it attractive to potential licensees (rather than the cost involved in setting up an entire business to make, market and sell the product).
- ❖ Freedom to move on to the next big business idea - if you do successfully license your product idea, you could receive royalties long after you've stopped working on the product!

Downside

- ❖ Finding the right licensee takes tenacity and determination, and can take a long time – don't quit your day job!
- ❖ Unless your product gets sold in a significant enough volume by the company to which you license it, the amount of royalties you receive can be low or non-existent.
- ❖ It's extremely difficult to get through the door of big companies to start a negotiation. That's partly why less than 3% of all patented ideas actually make it to market through licensing agreements

Building Your Vision

The best way to generate a good business model is to use the "Business Model Canvass". Go online (www.businessmodelgeneration.com/canvas) and print a Business Model Canvass. It's best to have a few copies because your ideas will change as you do Market Research. The canvass chucks your business idea into nine key chucks:

- ✓ **Key Partners** In order to optimize operations and reduce risks of a business model, organization usually cultivate buyer-supplier relationships so they can focus on their core activity. Complementary business alliances also can be considered through joint ventures, strategic alliances between competitors or non-competitors.
- ✓ **Key Activities** The most important activities in executing a company's value proposition. An example for Apple would be creating an efficient supply chain to drive down costs.
- ✓ **Key Resources** The resources that are necessary to create value for the customer. They are considered an asset to a company, which are needed in order to sustain and support the business. These resources could be human, financial, physical and intellectual.

Building Your Vision

- ✓ **Value Proposition** The collection of products and services a business offers to meet the needs of its customers. According to Osterwalder, (2004), a company's value proposition is what distinguishes itself from its competitors. The value proposition provides value through various elements such as newness, performance, customization, "getting the job done", design, brand/status, price, cost reduction, risk reduction, accessibility, and convenience/usability. The value propositions may be:
    i. Quantitative- price and efficiency
    ii. Qualitative- overall customer experience and outcome
- ✓ **Customer Relations** To build an effective business model, a company must identify which customers it tries to serve. Various set of customers can be segmented based on the different needs and attributes to ensure appropriate implementation of corporate strategy meets the characteristics of selected group of clients
- ✓ **Channels** A company can deliver its value proposition to its targeted customers through different channels. Effective channels will distribute a company's value proposition in ways that are fast, efficient and cost effective. An

Building Your Vision

organization can reach its clients either through its own channels (store front), partner channels (major distributors), or a combination of both.
✓ **Customer Segment** The different types of customer segments include:
   i. *Mass Market*: There is no specific segmentation for a company that follows the Mass Market element as the organization displays a wide view of potential clients.
   ii. *Niche Market*: Customer segmentation based on specialized needs and characteristics of its clients.
   iii. *Segmented*: A company applies additional segmentation within existing customer segment. In the segmented situation, the business may further distinguish its clients based on gender, age, and/or income.
   iv. *Diversify*: A business serves multiple customer segments with different needs and characteristics.
   v. *Multi-Sided Platform / Market*: For a smooth day to day business operation, some companies will

Building Your Vision

    serve mutually dependent customer segment. A credit card company will provide services to credit card holders while simultaneously assisting merchants who accept those credit cards.
- ✓ **Cost Structure** This describes the most important monetary consequences while operating under different business models. A company's DOC.

Classes of Business Structures:

    i. Cost-Driven - This business model focuses on minimizing all costs and having no frills. i.e. SouthWest

    ii. Value-Driven - Less concerned with cost, this business model focuses on creating value for their products and services. i.e. Louis Vuitton, Rolex

Building Your Vision

Characteristics of Cost Structures:

i. Fixed Costs - Costs are unchanged across different applications. i.e. salary, rent
ii. Variable Costs - These costs vary depending on the amount of production of goods or services. i.e. music festivals
iii. Economies of Scale - Costs go down as the amount of good are ordered or produced.
iv. Economies of Scope - Costs go down due to incorporating other businesses which have a direct relation to the original product.

- ✓ **Revenue Stream** The way a company makes income from each customer segment. Several ways to generate a revenue stream:
    i. *Asset Sale*: (the most common type) Selling ownership rights to a physical good. i.e. Wal-Mart
    ii. *Usage Fee* : Money generated from the use of a particular service i.e. UPS
    iii. Subscription Fees: Revenue generated by selling a continuous service. i.e. Netflix

Building Your Vision

 iv. *Lending/Leasing/Renting*: Giving exclusive right to an asset for a particular period of time. i.e. Leasing a Car
 v. *Licensing:* Revenue generated from charging for the use of a protected intellectual property.
 vi. *Brokerage Fees*: Revenue generated from an intermediate service between 2 parties. i.e.Broker selling a house for commission
 vii. *Advertising:* Revenue generated from charging fees for product advertising.

Building Your Vision

Once you have several copies of the canvass carefully answer the questions in each section. Remembers the previous lesson on the **Seven Basic Components of a Business Model** .

Carlton's Suggestions

- ✓ Take the time to understand the Seven Basic Components of a Business Model.
- ✓ Thoughtfully complete your business model canvass. Remember the first try isn't going to be the one, so be willing to create several drafts.
- ✓ Every business has its own business model. Be certain to select the business model option that suites your vision.

Building Your Vision

Step 3 Market Research

Building Your Vision

Now, that you have clearly identified the business you will be operating in you must prove your ideas with **Market Research**.

Marketing research can give a business a picture of what kinds of new products and services may bring a profit. For products and services already available, marketing research can tell companies whether they are meeting their customers' needs and expectations. By researching the answers to specific questions, small-business owners can learn whether they need to change their package design or tweak their delivery methods--and even whether they should consider offering additional services.

"Failure to do market research before you begin a business venture or during its operation is like driving a car from Texas to New York without a map or street signs," says William Bill of Wealth Design Group LLC in Houston. "You have know which direction to travel and how fast to go. A good market research plan indicates where and who your customers are. It will also tell you when they are most likely and willing to purchase your goods or use your services."

When you conduct marketing research, you can use the results either to create a business and marketing plan or to measure the success of your current plan. That's why

Building Your Vision

it's important to ask the right questions, in the right way, of the right people. Research, done poorly, can steer a business in the wrong direction. Here are some market-research basics that can help get you started and some mistakes to avoid.

Types of Market Research

Primary Research: The goal of primary research is to gather data from analyzing current sales and the effectiveness of current practices. Primary research also takes competitors' plans into account, giving you information about your competition.

Collecting primary research can include:

- Interviews (either by telephone or face-to-face)
- Surveys (online or by mail)
- Questionnaires (online or by mail)
- Focus groups gathering a sampling of potential clients or customers and getting their direct feedback

Building Your Vision

Some important questions might include:

- ✓ What factors do you consider when purchasing this product or service?
- ✓ What do you like or dislike about current products or services currently on the market?
- ✓ What areas would you suggest for improvement?
- ✓ What is the appropriate price for a product or service?

Secondary Research: The goal of secondary research is to analyze data that has already been published. With secondary data, you can identify competitors, establish benchmarks and identify target segments. Your segments are the people who fall into your targeted demographic-- people who live a certain lifestyle, exhibit particular behavioral patterns or fall into a predetermined age group.

Collecting Data

No small business can succeed without understanding its customers, its products and services, and the market in general. Competition is often fierce, and operating without conducting research may give your competitors an advantage over you.

Building Your Vision

There are two categories of data collection: quantitative and qualitative. Quantitative methods employ mathematical analysis and require a large sample size. The results of this data shed light on statistically significant differences. One place to find quantitative results if you have a website is in your web analytics (available in Google's suite of tools). This information can help you determine many things, such as where your leads are coming from, how long visitors are staying on your site and from which page they are exiting.

Qualitative methods help you develop and fine-tune your quantitative research methods. They can help business owners define problems and often use interview methods to learn about customers' opinions, values and beliefs. With qualitative research, the sample size is usually small.

Many new business owners, often strapped for time and money, may take shortcuts that can later backfire. Here are three pitfalls to avoid.

Building Your Vision

Common Marketing Mistakes

Using only secondary research. Relying on the published work of others doesn't give you the full picture. It can be a great place to start, of course, but the information you get from secondary research can be outdated. You can miss out on other factors relevant to your business.

Using only web resources. When you use common search engines to gather information, you get only data that are available to everyone and it may not be fully accurate. To perform deeper searches while staying within your budget, use the resources at your local library, college campus or small-business center.

Surveying only the people you know. Small-business owners sometimes interview only family members and close colleagues when conducting research, but friends and family are often not the best survey subjects. To get the most useful and accurate information, you need to talk to real customers about their needs, wants and expectations.

Building Your Vision

Carlton's Suggestions

- ✓ Base on your Business Model Canvass generate a Market Research survey.
- ✓ Be diligent in your questioning. If you designed a Business Model for your customer they will become phenomenal paying customers.
- ✓ Revisit your initial Business Model. Take what you learn from the market to adjust any key components of the canvass. You may have to do this many times before you know what the market wants.
- ✓ With your new canvass create an elevator pitch. A 60 word explanation of your business. This will prepare you for investors and future business relationships.

Building Your Vision

Step 4 Creating an One Page Business Plan

Building Your Vision

The One Page Business Plan methodology is the fastest, easiest way to write a plan. Using key words and short phrases plans can be created for a company, business unit, department, project or program… on a single page. This methodology focuses everyone in your company on what is important and critical for success!

Vision:

> What are you building? Write out the vision you created in the first chapter.

Mission:

> Why does this business exist? Write out the Mission Statement from chapter one.

Building Your Vision

Objectives

What will you measure? Clients, Assets, Relationships, Cash Flow ect.

Goals establish where you intend to go and tell you when you get there. They help improve your overall effectiveness as a company — whether you want to increase your share of the market, for example, or improve your customer service. The more carefully you define your goals, the more likely you are to do the right things and achieve what you wanted to accomplish in the first place.

Objectives are the specific steps you and your company need to take in order to reach each of your goals. They specify what you must do — and when.

Building Your Vision

Strategies

What will make this business successful over time? Base on what you learned from you business model and market research what technique will you use to run and grow your business? **Brand Promise**. What kind of relationship do you want to have with your customers? What problem do you want to solve for them? How will you make their lives better? This is what you want to describe in your brand promise, which will begin something like this: To be the best____ by _____. Or like this: To enhance our customers' _____ by _____.

Action Plans

What is the work to be done? Write a daily, monthly, and biweekly to-do list for your business. In the first months it's vital that you maximize time and effort to leverage your initial momentum.

Building Your Vision

Carlton's Suggestions

- ✓ Thoughtfully create this one page business plan. Include the information you gathered from you business model canvass and market research.
- ✓ Keep in mind that you are starting a small business, it is more important to make progress than have a lengthy professional plan at this stage.
- ✓ Be sure to include deadlines and milestone in your action plan.
- ✓ Congratulations your vision is building. Stay focus on your vision and remember to reinforce it daily with positive thoughts.

Building Your Vision

Step 5 Selecting a Business Structure

Building Your Vision

We will look at four forms of business ownership in this step:

1. Sole Proprietorships
2. Partnerships
3. Corporations
4. Limited Liability Companies

Forms of Ownership

For starters, it's important to take the time to review your life plan and business plan. What should emerge are answers to questions like:

- Do you want investors as shareholders in your company?
- Do you want to maintain control of the company if you have investors involved?
- Do you anticipate losses in the early stages that can be taken as tax benefits by shareholders?
- Do you want to avoid double taxation?
- Is there a great risk of liability associated with your specific business?

Building Your Vision

To help you determine the best structure for your business, I've put together an overview of several options. And remember, it's always best to work closely with an attorney and/or accountant to ensure you make the right choice. Legalzoom.com is an excellent source to help you with this process.

Sole Proprietorship

Sole proprietorships are a popular choice for many new business owners because so little is needed to set them up. Apart from local business licenses, there are minimal government fees and paperwork.

On the other hand, there are also considerable risks to consider—for example, your personal assets are vulnerable to creditors and other liabilities such as lawsuits. You also don't get to take advantage of certain tax breaks that are reserved for more formal business structures such as Corporations or Limited Liability Companies.

Most importantly, as a sole proprietorship, your company name is not protected. In other words, there is nothing to prevent another company from incorporating under your business name.

Building Your Vision

Partnerships

Similar to sole proprietorships, partnerships are extremely easy to set up and maintain, requiring no government fees or annual state paperwork. On the downside, you and your partners are each held fully responsible for all of your company's debts. This means if you or one of your partners defaults on a company loan, creditors can go after your personal bank accounts, property holdings and other assets to satisfy the entire loan.

As a partnership, you are also at a disadvantage when it comes to raising funds. For example, you cannot raise capital by selling stock, and private investors may be wary of investing in your company without personal liability protection. Finally, just as with sole proprietorships, your company name is not protected. This means any new or existing business could incorporate using your company name.

Corporations

Corporations are the standard for many businesses in today's market. The primary reason is that incorporating shields you and the members of your company from personal liability. In other words, if your business hits

Building Your Vision

hard times, creditors cannot go after your personal assets to make up for any company shortfalls.

But protection from personal liability is not the only benefit that comes with incorporating. The corporate business structure also offers significant tax savings, greater business flexibility, company name protection and increased opportunities for raising capital. You can also choose to set up your corporation as either a C-Corp or an S-Corp in order to take advantage of different tax options.

One thing to keep in mind - corporations do require some initial set up fees and a certain amount of regular maintenance. For example, you'll have to keep up-to-date corporate records as well as file an annual report with the state.

C Corporations

If you're ready for the big time and want to sell shares of stock in your business, consider a C Corporation. All publicly-traded companies are C Corporations which are considered a separate legal entity from the owners (also called the shareholders or stockholders) of the business. Because of this, the shareholders are not responsible for fees, liabilities and losses associated with the business.

Building Your Vision

The stock money and assets earned by the corporation belong to the corporation. Dividends are distributed to shareholders under the direction of the corporation's shareholder-elected Board of Directors. Stockholders then pay taxes on the earned dividends, and the corporation also pays taxes on all profits (known as "double taxation"). To become incorporated, you basically fill out the appropriate documents for the state and have all shareholders vote on overall corporate management, stock shares, the name of the company, business industry and other key guidelines.

As a C Corporation you will need to hold annual stockholder meetings and keep meticulous records to avoid legal and accounting problems. In addition, forming a corporation is an intricate process, so we highly recommend that you find a good attorney or consultant to assist you.

S Corporations

It is possible to avoid the double taxation of a C Corporation by forming an S Corporation. Here, the corporation's income is divided among all of the shareholders who report the earnings on their individual tax returns. This is a tax-efficient way to structure your business if you expect losses in the short term because the individual shareholders can report the losses on their

Building Your Vision

tax returns rather than paying the double taxation of the C Corporation.

The downside is that to become an S Corporation, you must run the company according to a fiscal calendar year, have less than 35 individual stockholders who are all U.S. residents, and have only one class of stock, in addition to other guidelines.

Limited Liability Companies

For many new entrepreneurs, choosing a business structure comes down to liability protection, tax savings and convenience. LLCs require fewer formalities and less on-going paperwork than corporations while offering the same personal liability protection and tax flexibility. Just as with a corporation, your company name is protected, and you and the other members of your company are shielded from creditors and other company liabilities such as lawsuits. But with an LLC, you only have to keep minimal company records, and there is no limit to the number of members your LLC can maintain.

Your company assets are only as good as your ability to protect them. This is especially true where intellectual property is concerned. Whether it's your company name, logo, latest invention or best-selling product, it's

Building Your Vision

imperative that you take certain steps to secure your ownership rights.

Carlton's Suggestions

- ✓ Take the time to review this section with any future team members.
- ✓ Visit your local government agency to see if any tax codes regulate your industry locally.
- ✓ As you weigh the marginal benefits keep the long term outcomes in mind.

Building Your Vision

Step 6 Key Business Assets

Building Your Vision

We will explore seven types of key assets in this step:

1. Website Address
2. Trademarks
3. Copyrights
4. Patents
5. Provisional Applications for Patents
6. Inventor's Logs
7. Confidentiality Agreements

Types of Key Assets

Website Address (domain name)

More than ever, businesses are turning to the web for both retail opportunities and online marketing. Key to establishing a website presence is securing a website domain name for your business. (An example of a domain name is **Facebook.com**)

There are a number of low-cost web services that will not only register your domain name, but also set up email and websites for you, complete with e-commerce capabilities such as godaddy.com and yola.com.

Building Your Vision

If you have a unique name for your company or product, be sure to immediately register it. If you discover someone else has already claimed the name you want, don't be discouraged. Often entrepreneurs allow their domain name registration to expire or are willing to sell their name to you at a reasonable price. Most domain name registration services provide contact information for domain name owners or offer a way to bid on domain names that are up for sale.

Trademarks

A trademark is one of the most important business assets you'll ever own. It's your brand name, your logo, or any other symbol that distinguishes your company or your company's goods from those of another manufacturer. By registering your trademark you go on record as the official owner of the mark, which gives you a significant leg up in court should a dispute over your right to use the mark ever arise. This comes in handy, for example, if you discover that another person or company is hurting your business reputation or causing confusion by using your mark to sell similar or cheaper-quality goods.

An owner of an unregistered mark may indicate ownership of a mark with the symbol "TM" for a trademark, or "SM" for a service mark.

Building Your Vision

In general, generic marks do not receive trademark protection because they are so general. On the other hand, owners of a registered mark are entitled to use the registration symbol ® in connection with their mark.

Copyrights

It's not uncommon for people to confuse copyrights with trademarks. Whereas trademarks are used to protect intellectual property such as company names, brands, logos and symbols, a copyright grants you exclusive legal rights to your creative work, which can include anything from literary or website content to musical or artistic compositions. In order to receive copyright protection for your work, your creation must be expressed in a tangible form such as a piece of writing or a recording. Once granted, a copyright prevents others from copying, performing or using your work without your permission.

Building Your Vision

Patents

If you have a bright idea, don't wait for someone else to turn it into a commercial success. You should quickly protect (assuming it is novel) so you can cash in first. The best way to protect your idea is to get a patent on it. A patent is a property right granted by the Government to an inventor "to exclude others from making, using, offering for sale, or selling the invention throughout the United States or importing the invention into the United States" for a limited time in exchange for public disclosure of the invention when the patent is granted. There are three kinds of patents, including: utility patents, design patents, and plant patents.

1. Utility patents may be granted to anyone who invents a useful process, a machine, an article of manufacture, or a composition of matter.

2. Design patents may be granted to anyone who invents a new, original, and ornamental design for an article of manufacture.

3. Plant patents may be granted to anyone who invents or discovers and asexually reproduces any distinct and new variety of plants.

Building Your Vision

A common misconception is that the patent gives its owner the right to make, use, or sell the invention. The patent only gives the owner the ability to *exclude others* from making, using or selling the invention. In a standard scenario, patents last for twenty years. The twenty years begins on the date that an application for a non-provisional or provisional patent was first filed. In deciding to patent your invention, we always recommend consulting a patent attorney.

Provisional Applications for Patents

A Provisional Application is a fast and easy way to temporarily protect your invention until you're ready to commit the time and money required to submit a full patent application. Think of it as a legal placeholder.

Because the application to secure patents is a lengthy and expensive process, the USPTO created a provisional patent which allows you to temporarily protect your invention. The non-provisional application establishes the filing date of your patent application and begins the examination process. A provisional application only establishes your filing date and expires automatically after one year.

You may file a provisional application if you are not ready to enter your application into the regular

Building Your Vision

examination process. A provisional application establishes a filing date at a lower cost for a first patent application filing in the United States.

A Provisional Application makes sure no one else rushes in and claims your invention while you're busy fine-tuning your design, securing funds, or testing your idea's market potential. A provisional application allows the term "Patent Pending" to be applied to your invention which can be useful in warding off any imitators.

But be careful. Provisional patents can come back to bite you later. You might find yourself limited or locked-in to what you describe in it, even though you've come up with additional improvements during your year-long provisional period.

If you go this route, we highly recommend that you at least include legitimate "claims," a key part of a formal patent. Otherwise, you should contact an attorney to patent your invention, or at least help you complete the application.

Inventor's Logs

The United States Patent and Trademark Office awards a patent to the first person who can prove they've invented a new product. An Inventor's Log Book helps you

Building Your Vision

establish that you were the first to develop your idea by recording the progress of your inventing. You should begin using an inventor's log the moment you conceive of an idea and continue to keep a detailed record of your activities as you develop your idea into reality.

Creating an Inventor's Log

In order to prove that you are the inventor of a specific invention, you should document and memorialize all information in an "inventor's log". U.S. Patent requires that you are the inventor of any invention claimed in a patent application and keeping an inventor's log may prove invaluable should you ever need to substantiate inventorship. A patent log also can be valuable if you need to prove that you were the first to invent a particular invention.

The inventor's log is literally a diary. The first entry should be posted when you conceive of your idea. This first entry should describe the invention, how you came upon it, the place, the circumstances, and any preliminary conceptual details. As you develop your invention, include in your inventor's log all engineering and testing data, drawings, research data, as well as any information related to similar products or patents you discover. It's also important to record the names of

Building Your Vision

anybody to whom you disclose your idea and the details relating to any such disclosures or meetings.

Your log entries should be kept in chronological order with entries posted one after the other on consecutively numbered pages, written in pen, and dated. Entries can take the form of strictly text, or could be drawings, or both. If you finish an entry partway down a page, do not start the next entry on the next page, rather post entries one right after the other in contiguous order. It is also beneficial to have an unbiased witness sign and date an entry if such a witness is conveniently available. It's important that you select a logbook with pages that cannot be added or subtracted without it being evident.

Should anyone else participate in the development of the invention, it's very important that you detail the contribution and clarify whether or not this participation resulted in an activity of inventorship or not. In order for a patent to be valid, all inventors must be named on the application.

Keep your notebook or notebooks in a secure location, and regularly photocopy or scan entries to keep a complete second copy of the log should the original get damaged or lost. Keep the copy in a separate location.

Building Your Vision

Confidentiality Agreements

Anytime you are considering exposing some of your company's secrets, whether it is a customer list, business process or financial data that you want to keep out of the hands of the competition, it is critical that you safeguard this information. With a Confidentiality Agreement, also called a Non-Disclosure Agreement or NDA, you can do just that. Typically, there are two types of NDAs: "One-Way" and "Mutual." When you hire a new employee or offer information to a potential business partner, a one-way NDA provides the protection you need in case the potential employee or business partner decides not to come onboard or engage you in business. When information is being passed both ways, each party should sign a mutual NDA.

Building Your Vision

Carlton's Suggestions

- ✓ Work with a trusted lawyer to select the structure that best suits your life. If you are not ready to commit to the tax obligations of a company you may want to file a "Doing Business As" with your local city government.
- ✓ Do your homework and remember to be very diligent as you handle legal matters.
- ✓ If you expect to net less than $800 per year it is best not to file.
- ✓ Review your assets and study the laws and regulations closely

Building Your Vision

Step 7 Finance Your Business

Building Your Vision

Thus far you have completed a vision and mission statement, learned the key metrics in running your business with the business plan model, and created a business plan. Now it is time to learn more about financing your business and basic business accounting.

This is a critical step. You've got to find funding for your business but ensure that it's the right *kind* of funding. Yes, there's the adage, "beggars can't be choosers," but the fact is, you must be selective and smart when seeking money for your startup or it could turn your dream business into a nightmare.

To identify which form of financing is just right for you, think about your long-term personal and business goals and the type of business you're planning to launch.Money comes in many forms, from tapping credit cards and taking equity out of your home to government grants and high net worth "angel" financing.

Building Your Vision

We will tackle seven ways to fund your business in this step:

1. Bootstrapping
2. Debt Financing
3. Grants
4. Friends and Family
5. Angel Investors
6. Factoring
7. Venture Capitalists

Building Your Vision

Ways to Fund your Business

Bootstrapping

Look no further than yourself to find the funding you need - perhaps using your savings, your initial revenues, credit cards, equity pulled from your home, etc.

Upside

- You maintain complete financial and operational control over your business.
- No equity-holders to pay off if the company hits it big.
- If you are able to use savings, you won't have monthly payments to add to your business expenses.

Downside

- If the business fails, you may face a lot of personal debt.
- Depending on the source of your personal capital, you may end up paying a high interest rate (if you use a credit card), or you may miss out on earning interest (if you use savings).

Building Your Vision

- Typically, this form of funding limits the amount of money you have for strategic purposes and the rate of growth of your business can be significantly slowed down as it starves for cash.

Debt Financing

Debt financing requires that you qualify for a traditional bank loan (not common for raw startups), or that you find a bank that can provide you a loan with a SBA guaranty.

Before you land a loan, you need to understand how to maximize your odds for success in landing a loan. The lending process is inherently a tough one, but it's also a system that has been the catalyst of success for many small businesses. In fact, some entrepreneurs would say that their relationship with their banker has been the pivotal ingredient to growth.

Upside

- You don't have to give up equity, proceeds or control in order to get funded.
- You build a powerful relationship with your banker that can open up additional forms of debt financing you may need down the road.

Building Your Vision

Downside

- ❖ Bank loans typically go to existing small businesses with 2 years of history and credit.

- ❖ You must pay interest, and if you don't keep up with your loan payments, you could find yourself in a tough spot with the bank.

- ❖ You may be required to provide personal collateral, such as your home, to obtain the loan.

Grants

Grants are special programs designed to fuel the innovative fires of small businesses, and typically target specific groups or types of businesses, such as technology businesses, veteran-owned businesses, women-owned businesses and minority-owned businesses.

Upside

- ❖ You don't pay interest - grants are essentially "free money."

- ❖ Potential investors (should you be seeking additional funding) love the "leverage" that grants provide.

Building Your Vision

Downside

- ❖ The competition is stiff for grants, and grant writing (applying for the grants) is an art form, so you may want to find a grant writer to help you.
- ❖ How you can use grant funds is strictly defined by the organization that provides them

Friends and Family

Just like it sounds, raise money from people you know well, either in exchange for equity or as a loan to be repaid.

Upside

- ❖ This option has the fewest contractual strings attached, although you should still draw up a contract to protect your friend's or family member's investment.
- ❖ Funds are typically available quickly.

Building Your Vision

Downside

- ❖ This is usually a limited, one-time source of funding.

- ❖ You are spending your friend's or family member's money - so do so wisely, and be prepared to deal with the consequences if your business does not succeed.

Resource

To better manage loans between friends and family, Circle lending provides a full range of services for managing financial transactions between private parties.

Angel Investors

Angel investors are individuals who invest in companies at an early stage in exchange for equity and the chance to help guide the company. In contrast, venture capitalists invest as a profession and generally on behalf of other investors.

Building Your Vision

Generally one is ready to approach angels when they have exhausted their friends and family but are not yet ready to approach venture capitalists for money.

Approach angels if you are looking for large amounts ($25K to $1M) of "smart money" - the people who provide this form of funding have already "made it big" in their own careers and can help guide you to do the same.

Upside

- ❖ Angels invest more than money - they provide mentoring and contacts.
- ❖ Angels are patient about their investment.
- ❖ There are no monthly payments with this type of financing - angels make their money when you achieve your business' exit strategy.

Downside

- ❖ Angels are difficult to find.
- ❖ Angels deserve regular and thorough reporting, which can take up valuable time.
- ❖ You are giving up equity in your company.

Building Your Vision

Factoring

Factoring is where the financial institution (factor) advances the entrepreneur money against proceeds from the entrepreneur's outstanding accounts receivables. Factoring firms generally are paid a percentage of the invoice's value.

Upside

- Provides funds quickly, when they might not otherwise be available.
- Helps companies with an unsteady and unbalanced cash flow.

Downside

- Factoring requires increased accounting oversight and administration.
- A substantial "cost of money" is involved in factoring. A hefty portion of your receivables will go the way of the factoring firm.
- Your customers are actually paying a factoring company rather than you.

Venture Capitalists

Building Your Vision

Venture capitalists are individuals or companies with large amounts of capital to invest and expect higher returns.

Use Venture Capitalists if you already have a great track record in your field or as an entrepreneur, and if you have a business concept that will require a lot of money ($250K to $10s of millions) and will have a rapid growth curve.

Upside

- ❖ VCs invest smarts and networking, in addition to money.

- ❖ VCs typically have more money available if you need it to grow down the road.

Downside

- ❖ VCs typically only invest in established companies.

- ❖ You must be willing to give up significant control over major decisions for your company.

- ❖ You must have a "fast growth" company.

- ❖ You must have an aggressive exit strategy to sell your business or do an IPO within 5-7 years.

Building Your Vision

The Ten Accounting Equation

The accounting equation equates assets with liabilities and owners' equity:

Assets = Liability + Owners' Equity

Assets are things owned by the company — such as cash, inventory, and equipment — that will provide some future benefit. *Liabilities* entail future sacrifices that the company must make, such as paying bills or other kinds of debts. *Owners' equity* represents the portion of the company that actually belongs to the owner.

A basic rule of accounting is that the accounting equation must always balance. If assets exceed the sum of liabilities and owners' equity, then the company holds things that don't belong to anyone. If the sum of liabilities and owners' equity exceeds assets, then owners and creditors lay claim to things that don't exist.

Net income

Net income is called the *bottom line* because in many ways it's the sum total of accountants' work. To calculate net income, subtract expenses from revenues:

Revenues − Expenses = Net income

Building Your Vision

Revenues are inflows and other kinds of sales to customers. *Expenses* are costs associated with making sales. Accountants also sometimes need to add gains or subtract losses in net income; these gains and losses come from miscellaneous events that affect stockholder value, such as selling equipment at a gain or getting your factory destroyed by a mutated prehistoric survivor of the dinosaurs.

Cost of goods sold

For manufacturers and retailers, *cost of goods sold* measures how much the company paid — or will need to pay — for inventory items sold.

To compute a retailer's cost of goods sold, use the following formula:

Beginning + Inputs = Outputs

Cost of beginning inventory + Cost of purchases − Cost of ending inventory = Costs of goods sold

Here, a retailer's inputs are the cost of the purchases it makes. The outputs are the goods that were sold (recorded at cost, of course).

Building Your Vision

Contribution margin

Contribution margin measures how selling one item, or a group of items, increases net income. To calculate contribution margin, subtract variable costs from sales:

Total sales − Total variable cost = Total contribution margin

Contribution margin helps managers by explaining how decisions will impact income. Should you prepare a special order with a contribution margin of $100,000? Yes, because it will increase net income by $100,000. Should you prepare another special order with a contribution margin of *negative* $50,000? No, because it will decrease net income.

To compute contribution margin per unit, divide the total contribution margin by the number of units sold. Alternatively, you can calculate sales price less variable cost per unit:

Sales price − Variable cost per unit = Contribution margin per unit

To compute contribution margin ratio, divide contribution margin by sales, either in total or per unit:

Building Your Vision

$$\text{Contribution margin ratio} = \frac{\text{Total contribution margin}}{\text{Total sales}}$$

$$\text{Contribution margin ratio} = \frac{\text{Contribution margin per unit}}{\text{Sales price per unit}}$$

Cost-volume profit analysis

Cost-volume-profit (CVP) analysis helps you understand how changes in volume affect costs and net income. If you know sales price, variable cost per unit, volume, and fixed costs, this formula will predict your net income:

Net income = (Sales price – Variable cost per unit)(Volume) – Fixed costs

First, understand where this formula comes from. Consider how production volume affects total costs:

Total cost = (Variable cost per unit x Volume) + Fixed costs

Variable cost per unit is the additional cost of producing a single unit. Volume is the number of units produced. Fixed cost is the total fixed cost for the period. Net income is just the difference between total sales and total cost:

Net income = (Sales price x Volume) – Total cost

Building Your Vision

Combining these two equations gives you the super-useful formula for understanding how volume affects profits:

Net income = (Sales price × Volume) - Total cost

$$= (\text{Sales price} \times \text{Volume}) - \begin{bmatrix} (\text{Variable cost per unit} \times \text{Volume}) \\ + \text{Fixed costs} \end{bmatrix}$$

= (Sales price × Volume) − (Variable cost per unit × Volume) − Fixed costs

Net income = (Sales price − Variable cost per unit)(Volume) − Fixed costs

Not coincidentally, a critical part of this formula equals contribution margin — remember that sales price less variable cost per unit equals contribution margin per unit:

Sales price − Variable cost per unit = Contribution margin per unit

This formula lets you further simplify the CVP formula:

Net income = (Contribution margin x Volume) − Fixed costs

Break-even analysis

Break-even analysis helps you determine how much you need to sell in order to break even — that is, to earn no net loss or profit. To figure out the break-even point, use this formula:

Building Your Vision

$$\text{Break-even volume} = \frac{\text{Fixed costs}}{\text{Sales price} - \text{Variable cost per unit}}$$

Perhaps you recognize contribution margin in the denominator (Sales price – Variable cost per unit), allowing you to further simplify this formula:

$$\text{Break-even volume} = \frac{\text{Fixed costs}}{\text{Contribution margin per unit}}$$

To figure out the number of units needed to break even, just divide total fixed costs by contribution margin per unit.

Price variance

Price variance tells you how an unexpected change in the cost of direct materials affects total cost. Use this formula to compute price variance:

Price variance = (Standard price – Actual price) x Actual quantity

Standard price is the amount you originally expected to pay, per unit, of direct materials. *Actual price* is the real price you paid, per unit, for direct materials. The *actual quantity* is the number of units purchased and used in production.

Building Your Vision

Although the price variance formula focuses on the direct materials variance, you can easily adapt it to figure out the direct labor variance. To do so, replace standard price with the standard cost (per hour) of direct labor. Replace actual price with the actual cost (per hour) of direct labor. Then replace the actual quantity with the actual number of hours worked.

Quantity variance

The direct materials quantity variance measures how using too much or too little in direct materials affects total costs. Stinginess in using direct materials should decrease your costs. However, wasting direct materials should increase costs. Here's the formula:

Quantity variance = Standard price x (Standard quantity – Actual quantity)

Remember that standard price is how much you originally expected to pay, per unit, of direct materials. Standard quantity is the number of units of direct materials that you expected to use. Actual quantity is the number of units of direct materials that you actually used in production.

Building Your Vision

Future value

Future value measures how much a present cash flow will be worth in the future. For example, if you put $1,000 into the bank today, earning 6-percent interest a year, how much will you have ten years from now?

To solve these problems, many students use tables printed in textbooks or financial calculators. You can also solve these problems using the time value of money formula:

Future value = –Present value x (1 + interest rate)^{Years}

Present value measures how much money you receive or pay now. Make this figure positive if you're receiving the money and negative if you're paying the money out. Future value is how much you can expect to receive or pay in the future (again, positive for incoming cash, negative for outgoing cash).

The interest rate should be put in as the *annual* interest rate (rather than daily, monthly, or quarterly). The number of years is for the period of time between the date of the present value and the date of the future value, in years.

Building Your Vision

Therefore, if present value equals –$1,000, the interest rate is 6 percent, and the number of years is ten years.

Future value = –(–$1,000) x (1 + 0.06)^{10}

= $1,000 x (1.06)^{10}

= $1,000 x 1.791

= $1.791

The future value indicates that, if you put $1,000 away now, earning 6 percent, you can expect to receive $1,791 at the end of ten years.

Present value

Present value uses the same formula as future value.

Future value = –Present value x (1 + interest rate)^{Years}

Here's an example of how you can use this formula to compute the present value of a cash flow. Suppose that, four years from now, you want to have $5,000 (that's the future value). How much should you put into the bank today, earning 5-percent interest?

Building Your Vision

$$\text{Future value} = -\text{Present value} \times (1 + \text{Interest rate})^{\text{Years}}$$
$$\$5,000 = -\text{Present value} \times (1+0.05)^4$$
$$\$5,000 = -\text{Present value} \times 1.2155$$
$$\frac{\$5,000}{1.2155} = \text{Present value}$$
$$-\$4,114 = \text{Present value}$$

So if you put $4,114 into the bank today, earning 5-percent interest, then in four years you should have $5,000 to take out.

Here's a version of the formula to more directly compute present value:

$$\text{Present value} = -\frac{\text{Future value}}{(1+\text{Interest rate})^{\text{Years}}}$$

Building Your Vision

Carlton's Suggestions

- ✓ Master the Ten basic accounting formulas before seeking any funding. Making money is the lifeline of the business. Having a basic understanding of account will prove to be extremely valuable.
- ✓ Review the funding strategies and align your choice with your company's vision.

Building Your Vision

Step 8 Establish an Organizational Structure

Building Your Vision

An organizational structure consists of activities such as task allocation, coordination and supervision, which are directed towards the achievement of organizational aims. It can also be considered as the viewing glass or perspective through which individuals see their organization and its environment. An organization can be structured in many different ways, depending on their objectives. The structure of an organization will determine the modes in which it operates and performs.

Organizational structure allows the expressed allocation of responsibilities for different functions and processes to different entities such as
the branch, department, workgroup and individual.

Organizational structure affects organizational action in two big ways. First, it provides the foundation on which standard operating procedures and routines rest. Second, it determines which individuals get to participate in which decision-making processes, and thus to what extent their views shape the organization's actions. A company's structure is made up of management, employees of various levels, and executives. Larger companies have boards which regulates the function of the company.

Small companies can use a variety of organizational structures. However, a small company's organization

Building Your Vision

structure must be designed to effectively meet its goals and objectives, according to the Lamar University article titled "Organizational Structure" on its website. Types of organizational structure in management can include flat structures as well as functional, product and geographical-structured organizations.

Flat Organizational Structure

Many small companies use a flat organizational structure, where very few levels of management separate executives from analysts, secretaries and lower-level employees. Flat organizations work best when a company has less than 20 employees, especially if the company employs one or two employees per department. One advantage of using a flat organizational structure for management is that decisions can be made relatively quickly. The flat organizational lacks the typical bureaucracy of taller organizational structures--those with many levels of management.

Functional Organizational Structure

A functional organizational structure is centered on job functions, such as marketing, research and development and finance. Small companies should use a functional organization when they want to arrange their organizational structure by department. For example, a

Building Your Vision

small company may have a director, two managers and two analysts in the marketing department. The director would likely report to the Chief Executive Officer, or CEO, and both managers would report to the director. In addition, each manager may have an analyst reporting to them. A functional organizational structure works well when small companies are heavily project-focused. Directors can assign certain projects to managers, who can then divvy up tasks with their analysts. The department can then more effectively meet their project deadlines.

Product Organzational Structure

A product organizational structure has managers reporting to the president or head of the company by product type. Product organizational structures are primarily used by retail companies that have stores in various cities. However, stores in each city may still need a local human resources or marketing department to carry out functions locally. For example, a small department store company may have a vice president of sporting goods, housewares and general merchandise at the corporate office. One manager may report to each vice president. However, each manager may oversee the work of one or more field marketing employees who travel and handle local marketing stores in several states.

Building Your Vision

These field marketing employees may work for the sporting goods manager one week in League City, Texas, then do merchandising for the housewares manager another week in the Sugarland, Texas, market.

Geographical Organizational Structure

The Small Business Administration is responsible for defining small businesses in different industries. For example, in manufacturing, the SBA usually considers a company with 500 or fewer employees a small business. Point is, small businesses are still large enough to use a geographical organizational structure. A geographical organizational structure is when companies decentralize the functional areas. For example, unlike the product organizational structure, there may be a local marketing, finance, accounting and research development person based in each region. For example, a small consumer products food company may be large enough to place a marketing research manager and analyst in each of six different regions. This can be important because consumers in various areas have different tastes. Hence, a geographical structure will enable the company to better serve the local market.

Once you choose the `the organization that best suits your company you will create a startup team. Buy now you realize that starting your business is a series of

Building Your Vision

important decisions. It is important not to rush any of the choices. In business each choice is interwoven.

Carlton's Suggestions

- ✓ Select the organizational Structure that fits the dynamic of your product or service.
- ✓ Build an amazing team of leaders. Business is the manifestation of relationships. Your team will be one of the most important assets you have assuming you are not working alone.
- ✓ Create a system that will work in cycles; time is money. Free your time to lead and delegate task.

Building Your Vision

Step 9 Market and Sell

Building Your Vision

Branding is one of the most important aspects of any business, large or small, retail or B2B. An effective brand strategy gives you a major edge in increasingly competitive markets. But what exactly does "branding" mean? How does it affect a small business like yours?

Simply put, your brand is your promise to your customer. It tells them what they can expect from your products and services, and it differentiates your offering from your competitors'. Your brand is derived from who you are, who you want to be and who people perceive you to be.

Are you the innovative maverick in your industry? Or the experienced, reliable one? Is your product the high-cost, high-quality option, or the low-cost, high-value option? You can't be both, and you can't be all things to all people. Who you are should be based to some extent on who your target customers want and need you to be.

The foundation of your brand is your logo. Your website, packaging and promotional materials--all of which should integrate your logo--communicate your brand.

Building Your Vision

Brand Strategy & Equity

Your brand strategy is how, what, where, when and to whom you plan on communicating and delivering on your brand messages. Where you advertise is part of your brand strategy. Your distribution channels are also part of your brand strategy. And what you communicate visually and verbally are part of your brand strategy, too.

Consistent, strategic branding leads to a strong brand equity, which means the added value brought to your company's products or services that allows you to charge more for your brand than what identical, unbranded products command. The most obvious example of this is Coke vs. a generic soda. Because Coca-Cola has built a powerful brand equity, it can charge more for its product--and customers will pay that higher price.

The added value intrinsic to brand equity frequently comes in the form of perceived quality or emotional attachment. For example, Nike associates its products with star athletes, hoping customers will transfer their emotional attachment from the athlete to the product. For Nike, it's not just the shoe's features that sell the shoe.

Building Your Vision

Defining Your Brand

Defining your brand is like a journey of business self-discovery. It can be difficult, time-consuming and uncomfortable. It requires, at the very least, that you answer the questions below:

- What is your company's mission?

- What are the benefits and features of your products or services?

- What do your customers and prospects already think of your company?

- What qualities do you want them to associate with your company?

Do your research. Learn the needs, habits and desires of your current and prospective customers. And don't rely on what you think they think. *Know* what they think.

Because defining your brand and developing a brand strategy can be complex, consider leveraging the expertise of a nonprofit small-business advisory group or a Small Business Development Center.

Once you've defined your brand, how do you get the word out? Here are a few simple, time-tested tips:

Building Your Vision

- **Get a great logo.** Place it everywhere.

- **Write down your brand messaging.** What are the key messages you want to communicate about your brand? Every employee should be aware of your brand attributes.

- **Integrate your brand.** Branding extends to every aspect of your business--how you answer your phones, what you or your salespeople wear on sales calls, your e-mail signature, everything.

- **Create a "voice" for your company that reflects your brand.** This voice should be applied to all written communication and incorporated in the visual imagery of all materials, online and off. Is your brand friendly? Be conversational. Is it ritzy? Be more formal. You get the gist.

- **Develop a tagline.** Write a memorable, meaningful and concise statement that captures the essence of your brand.

- **Design templates and create brand standards for your marketing materials.** Use the same color scheme, logo placement, look and feel

Building Your Vision

throughout. You don't need to be fancy, just consistent.

- **Be true to your brand.** Customers won't return to you--or refer you to someone else--if you don't deliver on your brand promise.

- **Be consistent.** I placed this point last only because it involves all of the above and is the most important tip I can give you. If you can't do this, your attempts at establishing a brand will fail.

How to Stretch A Marketing Budget

Most small businesses have modest marketing budgets, which means you have to make every dollar count. Here are 5 ways to get big results from a small budget:

First, use your ads for more than just space advertising. Ads are expensive to produce and expensive to run. But there are ways to get your advertising message in your prospect's hands at a fraction of the cost of space advertising.

The least expensive is to order an ample supply of reprints and distribute them to customers and prospects every chance you get. When you send literature in

Building Your Vision

response to an inquiry, include a copy of the ad in the package. This reminds a prospect of the reason he responded in the first place and reinforces the original message.

Distribute ads internally to other departments--engineering, production, sales, customer service and R&D--to keep them up to date on your latest marketing and promotional efforts. Make sure your salespeople receive an extra supply of reprints and are encouraged to include a reprint when they write to or visit their customers.

Turn the ad into a product data sheet by adding technical specifications and additional product information to the back of the ad reprint. This eliminates the expense of creating a new layout from scratch. And it makes good advertising sense, because the reader gets double exposure to your advertising message.

Ad reprints can be used as inexpensive direct mail pieces. You can mail the reprints along with a reply card and a sales letter. Unlike the ad, which is "cast in concrete," the letter is easily and inexpensively tailored to specific markets and customer groups.

If you've created a series of ads on the same product or product line, publish bound reprints of the ads as a

Building Your Vision

product brochure. This tactic increases prospect exposure to the series and is less expensive than producing a brand new brochure.

If your ads provide valuable information of a general nature, you can offer reprints as free educational material to companies in your industry. Or, if the ad presents a striking visual, you can offer reprints suitable for framing.

Use your ads again and again. You will save money--and increase frequency--in the process.

If something works, stick with it. Too many marketers scrap their old promotions and create new ones because they're bored with their current campaign. That's a waste. You shouldn't create new ads or promotions if your existing ones are still accurate and effective. You should run your ads for as long as your customers read and react to them.

How long can ads continue to get results? The Ludlow Corp. ran an ad for its erosion-preventing Soil Saver mesh 41 times in the same journal. After 11 years it pulled more inquiries per issue than when it was first published in 1966.

If a concept still has selling power but the promotion contains dated information, update the existing copy--

Building Your Vision

don't throw it out and start from scratch. This approach isn't fun for the ad manager or the agency, but it does save money.

Don't over present yourself. A strange thing happens to some entrepreneurs when they get a little extra money in the ad budget: they see fancy four-color brochures, gold embossed mailers and fat annual reports produced by Fortune 500 firms. Then they say, "This stuff sure looks great--why don't we do some brochures like this?" That's a mistake. The look, tone and image of your promotions should be dictated by your product and your market--not by what other companies in other businesses put out.

Producing literature that's too fancy for its purpose and its audience is a waste of money. And it can even hurt sales--your prospects will look at your overdone literature and wonder whether you really understand your market and its needs.

Use "modular" product literature. One common advertising problem is how to promote a single product to many small, diverse markets. Each market has different needs and will buy the product for different reasons. But on your budget, you can't afford to create a separate brochure for each of these tiny market segments.

Building Your Vision

The solution is modular literature. This means creating a basic brochure layout that has sections capable of being tailored to meet specific market needs. After all, most sections of the brochure--technical specifications, service, company background, product operation, product features--will be the same regardless of the audience. Only a few sections, such as benefits of the product to the user and typical applications, need to be tailored to specific readers.

In a modular layout, standard sections remain the same, but new copy can be typeset and stripped in for each market-specific section of the brochure. This way, you can create different marketspecific pieces of literature on the same product using the same basic layout, mechanicals, artwork and plates. Significant savings in time and money will result.

Use article reprints as supplementary sales literature. Marketing managers are constantly bombarded by requests for "incidental" pieces of product literature. Engineers want data sheets explaining some minor technical feature in great detail.

Reps selling to small, specialized markets want special literature geared to their particular audience. And each company salesperson wants support literature that fits his

Building Your Vision

or her individual sales pitch. But the ad budget can only handle the major pieces of product literature. Not enough time or money exists to satisfy everybody's requests for custom literature.

The solution is to use article reprints as supplementary sales literature. Rather than spend a bundle producing highly technical or application-specific pieces, have your sales and technical staff write articles on these special topics. Then, place the articles with the appropriate journals.

Article reprints can be used as inexpensive literature and carry more credibility than self-produced promotional pieces. You don't pay for layout or printing of the article. Best of all, the article is free advertising for your firm.

Explore inexpensive alternatives for lead generation, such as banner advertising, organic search and PR. Many smaller firms judge marketing effectiveness solely by the number of leads generated. They are not concerned with building image or recognition; they simply count bingo-card inquiries.

New-product press releases lead the list as the most economical method of generating leads. Once, for less than $100, I wrote, printed and distributed a new-product release to 100 trade journals. Within six months, the

Building Your Vision

release had been picked up by 35 magazines and generated 2,500 bingo-card inquiries. Post all your press releases in a media or press section of your website. Optimize your press releases with key word phrases to draw more organic search traffic.

Do not overpay for outside creative talent. Hire freelancers and consultants whose credentials--and fees--fit the job and the budget.

Top advertising photographers, for example, get $1,000 a day or more. This may be worth the fee for a corporate ad running in Forbes or Business Week. But it's overkill for the employee newsletter or a publicity shot. Many competent photographers can shoot a good black-and-white publicity photo for $200 to $250.

When you hire consultants, writers, artists, or photographers, you should look for someone whose level of expertise and cost fits the task at hand.

Do it yourself. Tasks such as distributing press releases or creating simple squeeze pages can usually be done cheaper in-house than outside. Save the expensive agency or consultant for tasks that really require their expertise.

Building Your Vision

If you do not have a marketing manager or assistant, consider hiring a full-time or part-time administrative assistant to handle the detail work involved in managing your company's marketing. This is a more economical solution than farming administrative work out to the agency or doing it yourself.

Get maximum mileage out of existing content (text and images). Photos, illustrations, layouts and even copy created for one promotion can often be lifted and reused in other pieces to significantly reduce creative costs. For example, copy created for a corporate image ad can be used as the introduction to the annual report.

Also, you can save rough layouts, thumbnail sketches, headlines and concepts rejected for one project and use them in future ads, mailings and promotions.

Pay your vendors on time. Why? You'll save money by taking advantage of discounts and avoiding late charges when you pay vendor invoices on time. And, you'll gain goodwill that can result in better service and fairer prices on future projects.

Social Marketing

Leveraging the power of content and social media marketing can help elevate your audience and customer

Building Your Vision

base in a dramatic way. But getting started without any previous experience or insight could be challenging.

It's vital that you understand social media marketing fundamentals. From maximizing quality to increasing your online entry points, abiding by these 10 laws will help build a foundation that will serve your customers, your brand and -- perhaps most importantly -- your bottom line.

1. The Law of Listening
Success with social media and content marketing requires more listening and less talking. Read your target audience's online content and join discussions to learn what's important to them. Only then can you create content and spark conversations that add value rather than clutter to their lives.

2. The Law of Focus
It's better to specialize than to be a jack-of-all-trades. A highly-focused social media and content marketing strategy intended to build a strong brand has a better chance for success than a broad strategy that attempts to be all things to all people.

3. The Law of Quality
Quality trumps quantity. It's better to have 1,000 online

Building Your Vision

connections who read, share and talk about your content with their own audiences than 10,000 connections who disappear after connecting with you the first time.

4. The Law of Patience
Social media and content marketing success doesn't happen overnight. While it's possible to catch lightning in a bottle, it's far more likely that you'll need to commit to the long haul to achieve results.

5. The Law of Compounding
If you publish amazing, quality content and work to build your online audience of quality followers, they'll share it with their own audiences on Twitter, Facebook, LinkedIn, their own blogs and more.

This sharing and discussing of your content opens new entry points for search engines like Google to find it in keyword searches. Those entry points could grow to hundreds or thousands of more potential ways for people to find you online.

6. The Law of Influence
Spend time finding the online influencers in your market who have quality audiences and are likely to be interested in your products, services and business.

Building Your Vision

Connect with those people and work to build relationships with them.

If you get on their radar as an authoritative, interesting source of useful information, they might share your content with their own followers, which could put you and your business in front of a huge new audience.

7. The Law of Value
If you spend all your time on the social Web directly promoting your products and services, people will stop listening. You must add value to the conversation. Focus less on conversions and more on creating amazing content and developing relationships with online influencers. In time, those people will become a powerful catalyst for word-of-mouth marketing for your business.

8. The Law of Acknowledgment
You wouldn't ignore someone who reaches out to you in person so don't ignore them online. Building relationships is one of the most important parts of social media marketing success, so always acknowledge every person who reaches out to you.

9. The Law of Accessibility
Don't publish your content and then disappear. Be

Building Your Vision

available to your audience. That means you need to consistently publish content and participate in conversations. Followers online can be fickle and they won't hesitate to replace you if you disappear for weeks or months.

10. The Law of Reciprocity
You can't expect others to share your content and talk about you if you don't do the same for them. So, a portion of the time you spend on social media should be focused on sharing and talking about content published by others.

Building Your Vision

Carlton's Suggestions

- ✓ Be constant as you Market and sell your product or service.
- ✓ Uniformity builds word of mouth and your brand will thrive from attention to details
- ✓ Fine your unique talent and emphasize it as you build your brand.
- ✓ Take time to make a monthly marketing goal and stick with it.

Building Your Vision

Step 10 Run and Grow

Building Your Vision

Starting up a company is a stressful, yet exciting venture. As the founder, you are the heart and soul of your company. In the early stages, you are the main driving force behind everything the company accomplishes.

But as success ensues and your company starts expanding, too often the startup outgrows a young entrepreneur's individual development and abilities. And with these growing pains, you will have to make decisions in areas where you lack real experience, knowledge or self-awareness.

While expansion is what you are after, it is imperative a young entrepreneur prioritizes and recognizes the importance of personal growth. By doing so, the product and company will have a greater chance of success. The more control you take of your own growth, the better it will be for your company, your employees and your bottom line.

Here are six tips on how to grow with your company:

1. Surround yourself with trusted individuals.
I am not referring to your mom or best friend. Find a mentor with the experience and industry expertise you lack but desperately need. Check out local meetup groups, reach out to organizations like SCORE or search the web for forums that feature experts in your field.

Building Your Vision

2. **Take a deep breath.**
Don't rush into decisions, no matter how urgent they seem. Take time to reflect on all potential outcomes, and seek advice before you make any decisions. It also helps to research similar companies and examine case studies. The more information you have in your arsenal, the more likely the decision you make will be the right one.

3. **Reflect on the mistakes.**
When things go wrong or you use poor judgment, figure out how you could have made a better decision. This exercise will grow your character and help you approach similar situations more effectively.

4. **Set up clear communication channels.**
While it isn't always fun to hear complaints about your management style, it is necessary to keep on top of your company and employee morale. Make sure you have a system in place for employees to air grievances, as well as provide you a constant loop of feedback.

5. **Utilize an executive coach.**
Even with decades of experience, Google's Eric Schmidt found an executive coach and advocates that everyone else get one too. People evolve constantly, and in the fast-paced world of startups, a coach can help you focus on that growth.

Building Your Vision

6. Know yourself.

This job isn't easy. Lean on your closest relationships for support and develop your own sense of self. When you are comfortable in your own skin, you'll be a more mature leader.

Making a decision is one of the most powerful acts for inspiring confidence in leaders and managers. Yet many bosses are squeamish about it.

Some decide not to decide, while others simply procrastinate. Either way, it's typically a cop-out -- and doesn't exactly encourage inspiration in the ranks.

To avoid pining over what to do and what to skip, it can help to learn how to make better decisions. You'll be viewed as a better leader and get better results overall. Here are five tips for making quicker, more calculated decisions:

1. **Stop seeking perfection.** Many great leaders would prefer a project or report be delivered only 80% complete a few hours early than 100% complete five minutes late. Moral of the story: Don't wait for everything to be perfect. Instead of seeking the impossible, efficient decision makers tend to leap without all the answers and

Building Your Vision

trust that they'll be able to build their wings on the way down.

2. **Be independent.** Good decision makers are "collaboratively independent." They tend to surround themselves with the best and brightest and ask pointed questions. For instance, in a discussion with subject-matter experts, they don't ask: "What should I do?" Rather, their query is: "What's your thinking on this?" Waiting for committees or an expansive chain of command to make decisions could take longer. Get your information from credible sources and then act, swiftly.

3. **Turn your brain off.** Insight comes when you least expect it. Similar to suddenly remembering the name of an actor that you think you'd just plumb forgotten. The same happens when you're trying to make a decision. By simply turning your mind off for a while or even switching to a different dilemma, you'll give your brain the opportunity to scan its data bank for information that is already stored and waiting to be retrieved.

4. **Don't problem solve, decide.** A decision can solve a problem, but not every problem can be solved by making a decision. Instead, decision

Building Your Vision

making often relies more on intuition than analysis. Deciding between vendors, for instance, requires examining historical data, references and prices. But the tipping point often rests with your gut. Which feels like the right choice?

5. **Admit your mistakes**. If your feelings steered you wrong, correct the error and fess up. Even making the wrong decision will garner more respect and loyalty when you admit you've made a mistake and resolve it than if you are habitually indecisive.

Building Your Vision

Carlton's Final Suggestions:

- ✓ Allow your vision to pull your dreams forward. With hard work your vision and mission will come to you in due time.
- ✓ Remember to plan then plan again, but do not forget actions are just as important as intentions.
- ✓ It is not enough to want a business you must master the lessons in this book.
- ✓ Align every choice related to your business with your vision. Always follow your own muse.
- ✓ Seek advice alone the process. No one makes it alone we all stand on the shoulders of giants.
- ✓ Show gratitude and celebrate every lesson and failure. Many entrepreneurs get so wraped up in the successes they do not enjoy the odyssey.

Building Your Vision

Meet the Author

Carlton Reed is experienced in a multitude of areas, ranging from Business Management/ Administration to Sociology. At University Cal State Dominguez Hills, as a student of the Academy of Business Leadership (ABL) He participated in an intensive transformational business leadership course and graduated in 2009 from the program with honor. ABL has truly changed his life and provided him with a clearer vision to pursue his goals and aspirations. As a result of completing the ABL program in 2009, He began a quest to start businesses that help others.

Carlton was the CEO/Founder of the non-profit organization Reaching High Standards (RHS). RHS assist students in excelling in their academics. In order to reach high standards RHS focuses on communication, career development, tutoring, trust building, giving back, and promoting self confidence. RHS is committed to making a difference and encouraging students to strive for excellence. Carlton expresses strong passion for

Building Your Vision

society by his volunteer work in his community. In addition, his dedication to the "Youthink" of the Zimmer Museum at the Jewish Federation shows his passion for service. As CEO. and co. Founder of Teenzbuy.com; a virtual store for teenagers, Carlton constantly challenged to raise the standard for virtual retail and redefine his own limitations.

Carlton has learned after years of striving to excellence it is not his various honors nor above average experience that establishes him as a leader , but it is; his passion, determination, self starter and visionary work that are Carlton's most valuable assets.

Building Your Vision

Bibliography

"3 Essential Formulas for Business; Trust, Change and the 80:20 | Roller Coaster of Personal Development." *Roller Coaster of Personal Development 3 Essential Formulas for Business Trust Change and the 8020 Comments.* N.p., n.d. Web. 16 July 2013.

"Marketing." *Entrepreneur.* N.p., n.d. Web. 16 July 2013.

"Step 2: Choosing a Business Model." *Choosing a Business Model: Step 2 of 10 Steps to Open for Business.* N.p., n.d. Web. 16 July 2013.

www.ingramcontent.com/pod-product-compliance
Lightning Source LLC
Chambersburg PA
CBHW072211170526
45158CB00002BA/543